CRAZY BONES®
Play The Craze!

FUNNY BONES

Jokes, riddles, knock-knocks, and loads of laughs starring the fabulous Crazy Bones!

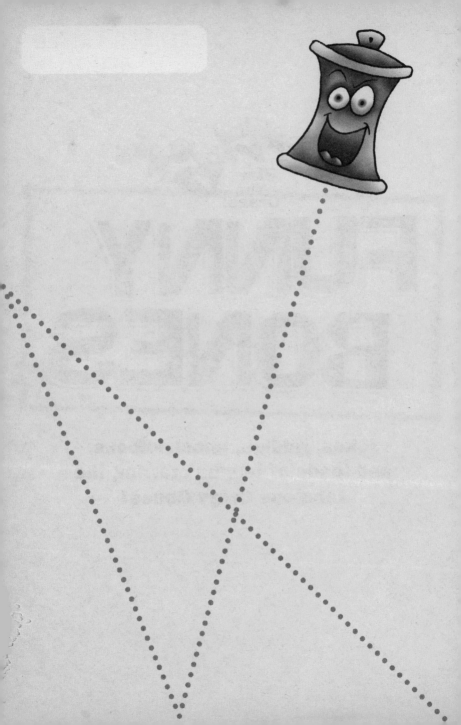

Play
The
Craze!

FUNNY BONES

Jokes, riddles, knock-knocks, and loads of laughs starring the fabulous Crazy Bones!

by Holly Kowitt

SCHOLASTIC INC.

New York   Toronto   London   Auckland   Sydney
Mexico City   New Delhi   Hong Kong

CRAZY BONES

are cool, collectable, wacky characters that come in dozens of colors, shapes, and styles. Each Crazy Bone has its own name, personality, and crazy sense of humor. And they all enjoy a good laugh! So keep reading...and go crazy for Crazy Bones!

ISBN 0-439-18019-8

12 11 10 9 8 7 6 5 4 3 2 1   0 1 2 3 4 5/0

Printed in the U.S.A.
First Scholastic printing, February 2000
Book design: Michael Malone

SHOW SOMEONE YOU REALLY SCARE

Why is it hard for Ghost to tell a lie?
You can see right through him!

Why did the teacher send Vampire
to the principal's office?
He had a bat attitude.

What do you say when Fang
asks you for a date?
"Fangs, but no Fangs!"

Why did Scary get an
answering machine?
He likes to scream his calls.

What does Floss want to be
when he grows up?
A fright attendant.

What does Lips say on his answering machine?

"Leave a message at the sound of the creep."

Why did Monster have an upset stomach?

He ate someone who disagreed with him.

What's Lagoon's favorite meal?
Bacon and Legs.

Why did Claws' mother come to school?
She had a parent-creature conference.

Why did Menace put worms
in his tuna sandwich?

Because cockroaches are too crunchy.

If Reggae was a zombie,
what would he wear?

Deadlocks.

JOKES THAT REALLY ROCK!

Why did the bee join Rocker's band?

To be the lead stinger.

Why did Heavy Metal put
strawberries in his guitar?

He wanted to have a jam session.

What kind of music group
is Stretch in?

A rubber band.

What did Ringo bring to
Thanksgiving dinner?

His own drumsticks.

What kind of music does
Brains like best?
Heavy Mental.

How did Music get on the radio?
She sat on it.

Rapper asks: "What kind of
music do mummies like?"
Answer: Wrap!

Why did Rock Star bring a hammer
into the recording studio?
He wanted a hit record.

Why did Music hold a
funeral for her radio?
The batteries were dead.

BONE APPETIT!

What does Frenchy get when
he takes airplanes?
Frequent Fryer Miles.

What do you get when
Melon Head goes boxing?
Fruit punch.

Why did Carmen Boneranda
go to the fruit store?
She was looking for a date.

How did Miss T. feel when
her cup got stolen?
Steamed!

What happens when Fudgy
gets into a fight?
He gets licked.

Why did Bone Cone become
a newspaper reporter?
To get the latest scoop.

Why did Toasty go to the doctor?
He was feeling crumby.

What did Chef say when he
spilled soup on himself?
"Lunch is on me!"

Why did the girl put Edison
in her lunchbox?

She wanted a light snack.

Why did Java get kicked out of
the restaurant?

They refused to serve coffee.

What does Eggy do when you
tell him a joke?

He cracks up.

What did Toasty say to the knife?

"Stop trying to butter me up."

BONE TO RUN!

Why did Dummy bring a rope
to the football game?

He wanted to tie up the score.

Why did Dopey wear a baseball mitt
to the railroad station?
He was hoping to catch a train.

Coach: How many feet are
in a football field?
Answer: It depends who's standing on it!

How does Cleats say good-bye?
"Gotta run!"

Why does Wheels eat fast food?
He likes to eat and run.

When Timid plays baseball,
what kind of balls does he hit?
Shy balls.

Why did Cleats go to the White House?
He wanted to run for President.

How did Crazy Bug learn to be
a demolition derby driver?
He took a crash course!

How did Horn feel when his favorite
team won the big game?
He was blown away.

GAGS TO MAKE YOU GAG!

Why can't Rubbish get a date?
Because no one will take him out.

What newspaper does Swirly read?
The Toilet Paper.

Why did the Blob vomit into the phone?
The recording said,
"Heave a message at the beep."

What's backward about Big Foot?
His feet smell and his nose is running.

What did the judge say when
he saw Stinky?
"Odor in the court!"

JUST KNOCKING

Knock-knock.
Who's there?
Fang.
Fang who?
You're welcome!

THE NATURE COLLECTION

Available in:

N136
Rosso Verona

Available Exclusively at

Knock-knock.
Who's there?
Rapper.
Rapper who?
Rapper in a towel—she's all wet!

Knock-knock.
Who's there?
Pig Tails.
Pig Tails who?
Pig Tails me some pretty
awful knock-knock jokes!

Knock-knock.
Who's there?
Brains.
Brains who?
Brain's coming down hard—
bring an umbrella!

Knock-knock.
Who's there?
Weirdo.
Weirdo who?
Weirdo you get all these
terrible knock-knock jokes?

Knock-knock.
Who's there?
Boo.
Boo who?
Stop being a Cry Baby
and open the door!

BONE TO BE WILD!

Why does Hiss like going to the movies?
He enjoys the Snake Previews.

What do you say when Tentacle
asks you for a date?
You've got to be squidding!

Why did Baldy put a rabbit on his head?
He needed the hare.

Where does Puppy leave his car?
In a barking lot.

Why did Nautilus visit an ant farm?
He had some bugs to work out.

Why did Oink turn down a
party invitation?
He wasn't in the mud.

Where does Freddie Frog
buy his clothes?

At a hopping mall.

What does Miss Froggy order
at McDonald's?

A burger and flies.

What's Sharky's favorite candy?
Jawbreakers.

What did Jaws say to the swimmer?
"It's been nice gnawing you."

A STAR IS BONE!

Why doesn't Bikini Baby like the new dance club on the moon?

It has no atmosphere.

Where can Orbit go for a cup of coffee?
Starbucks.

What do you get when you cross
Cowboy with a meteor?
A shooting star.

What kind of music group
can aliens join?
A Martian band.

Why did it take Cyclops eight hours
to finish two videos?

He wasn't very hungry.

iT'S NOT THE HEAT, iT'S THE STUPiDiTY!

What kind of weather does Chubby like?
Heavy showers.

Why does Head Case carry an umbrella?
In case of a brainstorm.

What is Ole's weather report?
"Chili today, hot tamale."

What does Fan do when he
goes to the beach?
The wave.

Who does Skipper call when
he needs a ride?
A taxi crab.

I WAS ONLY CHOKING!

How does Stewie relax?
He climbs into a hot tub.

Why did Flash turn red?
*He was embarrassed to change
in front of everyone.*

How did Cool Dude get so cool?
He has lots of fans.

What are the only two things Pudge
can't have for breakfast?

Lunch and dinner!

What kind of car does
Funny Bones drive?

A jokeswagon.

What do you call Rat Fink when he crosses a muddy street twice?

A dirty double-crosser.

What do you get when Hulk walks
through your garden?
Squash.

What do you call Attila when he's
carrying a 50-gallon Super Soaker?
Sir.

What will it say on Robo's tombstone?
Rust in peace.

What's Four Eyes' normal eyesight?
20-20-20-20!

Why does Siesta always whisper?
So he doesn't wake his sleeping bag.

Why does Fly Boy wear a blue cape?
His green one is at the cleaners.

Why did Dopey put a clock
under his desk?
He wanted to work overtime.

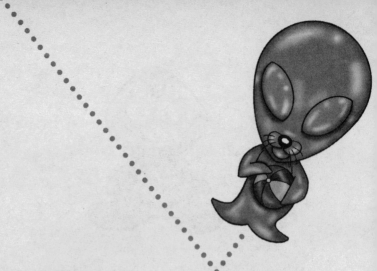

Why did Ar Ar put his bed
in the fireplace?

He wanted to sleep like a log.

Why doesn't Nimble have many friends?

He's a real drip.

Why did Sheriff Bones arrest his belt?
It held up his pants.

What do you get when Blades
goes on safari?
In-lion skating.

What does Cable Guy eat dinner on?
A satellite dish!

What does Pssst get told most often?
"Say it, don't spray it!"

JUST SCHOOLING AROUND

Why did Striker bring a
hammer to school?

*His teacher said it was
time to hit the books.*

What does Gigabone like to
do after school?
Come home and crash.

What kind of sentence did
the judge give Inky?
A year in the pen.

Why was Snippy kicked out of school?
He cut class!

Why did Bad Boy miss his teacher?
His aim was bad.

What kind of test do you give Corked?
A pop quiz!

Why did the boy bring King Bones
to math class?
He needed a ruler.

Why did Goodie Goodie put her exam
in the swimming pool?
She wanted to test the waters.

Bookworm: How do you make
a library bigger?
Answer: Add a few stories!

What kind of friend does Inky like best?
Pen Pals.

Why did Spinner put a notebook
in the wash?
To get a clean sheet of paper.

MiX AND MATCH BONES

What do you get when you cross
Weirdo and Cry Baby?
An Unidentified Crying Object.

What do you get when you cross
Mac and Snooze?

A burger alarm.

What do you get when you cross
Veggie and Orbit?

Onion rings.

What do you get when you cross
Crazy Bug and Planet Go Go?
A parking meteor.

What do you get when you cross
Telebone with a pelican?
A big bill.

What do you get when you cross
Wheels and Funny Bone?
Someone who's wheely funny.

What do you get when you cross
Clown and Bootz?
The Greatest Shoe on Earth.

Knock-knock.
Who's there?
Java.
Java who?
Java good knock-knock joke?
I'm all out...

Knock-knock.
Who's there?
Telebone.
Telebone who?
Tell a bone a knock-knock joke,
   and he'll break up!

Knock-knock.
Who's there?
Dynomite.
Dynomite who?
Dyno might know some good
   knock-knock jokes.

Knock-knock.
Who's there?
Fish Bowl.
Fish Bowl who?
Fish bowl in leagues under the sea!

Knock-knock.
Who's there?
Bookworm.
Bookworm who?
Book wormed his way into
this knock-knock joke!

Knock-knock.
Who's there?
Eel.
Eel who?
Eel kill me if I tell another
knock-knock joke!

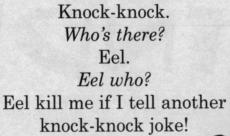

63

THE END!

(And we're not joking!)